Beaut the Spotlight

Edited by Fran Dworak

2019

Beautiful Images in the Spotlight
Poems copyright © 2019 by each author listed with a poem.
All rights reserved. With the exception of excerpts this book may not be reproduced without prior written permission from editor/author, Fran Dworak

Write Mary Frances Dworak
Morristown, NJ 07960

Published by Kindle Direct Publishing KDP.amazon.com
To order additional copies of this title, see Amazon.com
Special Edition 2019
ISBN: 9781096551010

Dedication:

This collection of writings is dedicated to a beautiful woman and spiritual friend. Paula Jones is a deeply loved member of two worshipping communities. She is held close by a sustaining ribbon of care and compassion that, by touching each -- connects.

Prayer Shawl Blessing by Fr. Peter Krebs:

To expressly bestow a special blessing on someone we hold dear in our minds and hearts, a "prayer shawl," having been knit by members, is presented with love. This practice has been a tradition of the Christian Community. On Easter Sunday a "prayer shawl" was blessed and placed on Paula Jones' shoulders. The community's blessing prayer was:

"Paula, as you wrap yourself in the comfort of this shawl, may you deeply feel the reassurance of your community's prayer of love and respect for you. Through the grace of God's blessing within this shawl may you know your importance, as well as the inspiration you bring to so many in our Christian Community, and outside it. May God bless you with patience in your healing process and trust in those who minister to you.

May God's healing grace come to you. May it heighten your awareness of His love for you and His presence with you on your journey. May you always feel our prayer, our blessing, our love; and may our respect surround you as this shawl comforts and strengthens you with God's closeness. God bless you and keep you close to his healing heart - always."

Editor's Note:

In our quest to help in unburdening a faithful friend's mind, a number of us have gathered our own original writings into this collection centered on beauty in the creation and in soulful people, like Paula, who surround us.

May these words be a shawl of comfort to all who pause to reflect. Through a diversity of poetic styles, the poems, sewn together, become a colorful patchwork quilt. Here twenty writers treat us with unique experiences as they share their appreciation of the creation. Their words come alive in poetry, connecting us to each other in a communion of thoughts and love. As you wind your way in an expansion of passion for the creation, look for deeper meanings that may be found as though hidden in a nested Russian doll

Writers reflect on beauty and sensations that have been etched in their hearts and minds, never to be forgotten. See beauty in mountains with unending views of emerald reflecting oceans. See beauty in birds, flowers, trees, in all seasons, see beauty where all priestly people laud the fullness of all life. See beauty where ordinary miracles are overlooked in an ordinary day, and where valued wisdom and goodness eclipse malice.

Many have contributed to this book; the names of the authors are listed on the next page and later in bylines with their writing. Notice the "heart" page of beautiful images, many community members have provided its contents. Others have supported this project in various ways including communication and proofreading.

Poetry Authors

Rev. Peter Krebs

Margaret A. Dukes

Frank Dworak

Louise Easton

Diane Gallo

Maureen Grant

Joan Gunning

Pat Koman

Susan Kraus

Don Kuhn

Norman Lubeck

Joanne McAneny

Margaret McCaffrey (Schuloff)

Karen McGregor

Julie O'Connell

Maryanne Pennella

Jules Romond

Linda Stamato

Camille Yates

Fran Dworak, Writer and Editor

"The beauty you see in me is a reflection of you." Rumi

"The power of imagination makes us infinite" by John Muir

*"Beauty is eternity gazing at itself in a mirror
But you are eternity **and** you are the mirror"* Kahlil Gibran from *"The Prophet."*

"Every particular in nature, a leaf, a drop, a crystal, a moment of time is related to the whole, and partakes of the perfection of the whole." Ralph Waldo Emerson

With ❤ Heart ❤ a Spotlight on Beauty:

She showers love on her daughter ❤ She is a favorite flower girl ❤ She has trust - in Me ❤ She walks with beauty ❤ She has fearless conviction in speaking truth ❤ She has a joyful heart ❤ She is meditative ❤ She likes wearing a hibiscus in the hair ❤ She is a caring supportive nanny ❤ She is a sweet singer ❤ she is happy to give ❤ she is a calm advocate ❤ She has quiet grace ❤ She is a spiritual Christian ❤ She has humble wisdom ❤ She faithfully trusts whether in sickness or health ❤ She is as bright as daffodils ❤ She is happy to give ❤ She radiates from her eyes ❤ She prefers red or navy blue ❤ She lovses MercyMe ❤ She loves songs of praise ❤ She loves words that please ❤ She loves memories of Trinidad ❤ She burst with pride on seeing Jamellia in her graduation gown ❤

Table of Contents

Dedication: iii

Prayer Shawl Blessing *by Fr. Peter Krebs* v

Editor's Note: vii

Poetry Authors... ix

With ♥ Heart ♥ a Spotlight on Beauty: xi

They Share Beauty *by Fran Dworak* 1

Measuring Love *by Karen McGregor* 2

Joyful Chorus *by Fran Dworak*........................ 3

Amaryllis *by Don Kuhn* 4

Grace Is .... *by Joan Gunning* 5

Mountains to Sea *by Fran Dworak* 6

Testimony *by Jules Romond* 7

Breathing While Eighty *Inspired by Don Quinn* 8

The Light of Life *by Fran Dworak* 9

Resurrection *by Diane Gallo* 10

Ripples of Spring *by Joanne McAneny* 11

Valentine Poem *by Margaret A. Dukes*............. 12

First Steps (For Rosemary) *by Don Kuhn* 13

Dance with Beauty *by Fran Dworak*................ 14

Unitarian Poem *by Margaret A. Dukes*............. 15

The Photographer *by Julie O'Connell* 16

Transformation *by Margaret A. Dukes*............. 18

Kiss of the Flower *by Frank Dworak* 19

Beauty and the Beach *by Maryann Pennella* 20

Time *by Joan Gunning*............................... 22

Well of love *by Louise Easton* 23

Faith and Grace at EAME *by Linda Stamato* 24

Mother's Day Poem to the World *by Margaret Dukes*.. 25

Cuckoo-bum-castle *by Fran Dworak* 26

Poem of the Morning *by Margaret A. Dukes*...... 27

Minds-Eye Wings *by Fran Dworak* 28

The Painter *by Pat Koman*........................... 29

On Seeing Warhol at the Whitney *by Julie O'Connell* 30

Oregon Spring *by Don Kuhn* 32

The Robins of Spring *by Frank Dworak* 33

She Walks with Grace *by Maureen Grant* 34

The Flower of Spring *offered by Norman Lubeck* 35

Early Summer Day *by Don Kuhn* 36

Meditation by the Pool *by Camille Yates* 38

Monsoon Listening *by Susan Kraus* 39

Digging Dahlias *by Don Kuhn* 40

Tucson Poem *by Susan Kraus* 41

Autumn Prayer *by Don Kuhn* 42

Winter Wonder *by Frank Dworak* 44

Late Autumn *by Margaret McCaffrey* 45

Grand Old Oak Tree *by Fran Dworak* 46

I Wonder as I Wander *by Margaret McCaffrey* 47

One Lifetime *by Fran Dworak* 48

Beautiful Images in the Spotlight

They Share Beauty *by Fran Dworak*

Imagine an animated bouquet in perfumed
balmy air
Unhurried by Trinidadian time
Where a garden is gaily dressed to compete for
the Creator's attention

The breeze and the bees caress a pink hibiscus
Rallying its greenery to frolic energetically
There where the jasmine, gardenia,
Magenta bougainvillea sway in synchrony
Seducing a tufted coquette to feed on seeds

Heavenly essence emerges from coaxing
Sweet minerals from sanctified nurturing soil
As proudly the blooms boast fragrance in their
grace

And you
You are invited to linger at this table with the
Creator
To indulge in the beauty
A patio bench chair is there

Measuring Love *by Karen McGregor*

(Sister of Linda Stamato)

Why can't the fullness, freeness
And depth of love
That is being given—be felt?

Why can't the strength of the moment
Be the way of measuring
 —why always the length?

Why can't the receiving be as strong
As the giving?

Look deep and see the love and
Sharing—
Know it; feel it; want it;
And be safe.

Joyful Chorus *by Fran Dworak*

A welcoming smile below hopeful
eyes reveal her soulful nature.
An ineffable light shines out
Her spirit beautifully naturally shared.

I am drawn closer.

The music wafting and lifting
she sings: "I Can Only Imagine,"
filling her proud and confident body.
Clicking her fingers, she sways to the beat.

I am drawn closer.

A divine image, she, sitting with her creator
at the center alongside loving friends,
rapt in those songs of grace, where
hope is not cold in beating hearts.

I am drawn closer.

I join the joyful fine chorus, those voices
accompanied by the galvanizing gospel five
overflowing the room with holy liveliness.
"You are treasured, you are beautiful."

Amaryllis *by Don Kuhn*

Hidden within you,

But awakened to life as warm water

Flooded around you,

You thrust your buds up proudly

Impatient to proclaim your beauty.

Now, two great trumpets, red-striped-white,

Stand poised on my desk

As if from some medieval balcony

To break the air with antique flourishes.

Though your trumpets are mute,

I hear them:

Their music floods my soul.

Will I break into bloom?

Grace Is .... *by Joan Gunning*

Grace can be a mystery
...only if we let it
Grace is all around us
...only if we look for it
Grace makes the world
A better place
...only if we recognize it
Living in and with Grace every day.
In a radiant smile
It's in her knowledge that
Jesus is always with her

Grace is a gift that must be opened
She has opened her gift
and shared
...Quiet strength
...Warm embrace
...Laughter and Joy
Because she is blessed
      So too, are We.

Mountains to Sea *by Fran Dworak*

I enjoyed that breeze in the universe of the trees
I left footprints on those mountain paths
There overlooking the emerald tropical sea
I tasted cool waters freely springing from
The Rock
Where miracles were meant for me.
Here, in stillness
I continue to be enthralled by
Creation's infinite view of the holy

Testimony *by Jules Romond*

The sky beckons the dogwood ethereal branches
upward, the tree seems to comply;
but for sturdy trunk and roots ensconced in dirt
there shall be no reply.

The flowers float above the ground and dance in the
breeze, although their quiet moments mesmerize.
The branch's profile gives us an unsymmetrical
snowflake, not unsympathetic to beauty;
but her pink sisters who are embarrassed
by this quality, blush behind this imagery
into that of a red sunrise.

What seems a pleasant site before our eyes
is actually testimony for the soul of the earth.

Breathing While Eighty *Inspired by Don Quinn*

Walk in nature alongside Don, join the ritual cleansing of lungs, mind and spirit. Authored by Fran Dworak.

Purposeful constancy is a necessity of life.
Inside the cottage's corner quarter,
in a routin'd response to new light, he rises.
Putting feet in shoes, donning his cap, his purpose a
vital called-for washing, cleansing, clearing the
remains of lungs nightly task. Whilst in the company
of wafting sweet honeysuckle, he paces the practiced
forest path, a green and periwinkle-blue palette, fully
indulging in the morning quiescent landscape, sky-
reflecting dawn on the high mountain lake. Pulling in
the cool elixir, he blows out the warm asphyxiator:
nature's balanced exchange.

Already a dinghy is racing aside, now lengthening
his stride for the morning's mis-match, filling his
awareness, replacing his notice, he hums the tune left
by last evening's Tchaikovsky performance.
Again at the beach, he passes white sheets raised
for the day's tacking, drawing an easy deep breath,
keeping the elated spring in his step, once more he
opens the cottage door.

The Light of Life *by Fran Dworak*

As a tide gently strokes
At the mountain lake shoreline
Seven early risers
Pose high with spine aligned
Alert, face east

Wait to witness a grand opening
An orange-red luminesce
The show: life's force.
Now with the lark ascending
Already singing
Prayerfully sparked senses respectfully salute

Worthy or unworthy
The source, the light, the spirit giver
Bursts Forth
Unveiling the shine on all
Surya Namaskar

Infused with a new energy, joined by
Mallards, five chicks in line, a wake behind
Friends in circle, turn, eyes engage
Palms alongside a heart beating, a bowing
Addressing the sacredness of the other
Namaste

Resurrection *by Diane Gallo*

The sun's rays have not yet opened the
morning clouds. Birds are wheeling and diving
in their early-morning frenzy.

I shuffle into the dark kitchen, not fully awake but
my mind's already focusing on the day's tasks...

Not wanting to turn on the lights to see the
dirty dishes in the sink, the crumbs on the floor,
the cat's empty dish.

And then the sun breaks through
piercing the clouds.

A bright ray of light shines into the room,
opening my eyes to a new way of seeing;
cleansing my soul,
shedding the old skin of yesterday.

I greet the new day with a fresh face, with a
hope that lifts my spirits sending them soaring.

      Soaring with the birds

Ripples of Spring *by Joanne McAneny*
(At Peter's Pond Reeves Reed Arboretum)

Babbling down a slight rocky incline,
Life giving water, clear and cool.
Nearby beautiful yellow flowering trumpets,
Announce the arrival of the soothing warmth
to come.

Admiring flecks of bright orange,
Gliding under sage green water lilies.
Like captured rays of sunshine,
Bringing light to the dark pond.

Strolling down a garden path,
One's spirits are lifted.
Signs of nature bring the promise of a
new beginning.--
For now we know the harsh frigid days
are past.

Valentine Poem *by Margaret A. Dukes*

It doesn't take the fastest route
it often misses the most scenic
Google maps doesn't help it.
It travels on the clearer
roads of honest communication,
avoids one-way streets,
takes wrong turns
then yields the right of way.
Derailed on its worst days
it goes beyond any temporary anger,
impatience, mistakes,
misunderstandings.
The transportation of love - endures
after the last stop.

First Steps (For Rosemary) *by Don Kuhn*

She stands up slowly locking
Reluctant knees, teetering a bit
Face serious. Can she relax
A knee to move forward
Or will that force her
Back to a crawl?
She lifts a foot, inches forward,
Makes a step, then, magically,
Lifts the other, a second step.
"She's walking," we cry –
A milestone reached.

How many "first steps"
Will there be? The first
picture painted. The first
book read. The first date.

How will those go for her?
From rigid swaying to confidence?
From timidity to assurance?
Will we cry, "She's done it!"
With comparable enthusiasm,
Accepting the less than perfect
Along the way?

Dance with Beauty *by Fran Dworak*

In a burst of emotion
In an explosion of suggestion
In the submittal to a beat
Life is moving us

We don't need feet to feel that beat
To click our fingers
To compete in the joy of the dance
On the street, in the gym, on the ballroom
floor
Dance is there in the lexicon of the world.

Whirling Dervishes pray
Hamlet a'stage avoids the epee
Matisse joyfully turns in framed life
Wheelchairs spin in the competition

Earth twirling in its space
Directs the daily dance
As we dreamy dancers *do* carry on
And on

Unitarian Poem *by Margaret A. Dukes*

Those red high-top converse sneakers
press the keys under the piano,
provide a visual to enhance the
upbeat classical prelude to my first Berkshire
Unitarian service.
The women's whole body is a grace note,
she plays with swollen fingers,
slight curved spine,
gray top knot.
Her hands, like small fish,
jump into the stream of the ivories
to create ecstasy
even scientists can't explain.
Is it also so
for every newcomer,
or old comer,
or was it just my body
that seemed to float on the gift of
togetherness her music evokes?
Isn't it something we all come for?

The Photographer *by Julie O'Connell*

Light falls unevenly

from a spot I can't see

And yet, you see it -

the warm brilliance

in darkness

the light crashing on

barren landscape

until shadows

fade it black.

You find the story

make the center

tell the sunshine

where it should fall

like God himself

separating light from darkness

on that first day.

Chiaroscuro

As if you have been

handcrafted for this task

Rembrandt revealing

and concealing

in contrast.

Isn't it like that

for all of us?

We are a mixture
of light and shadow
brightness and gloom
candles in a dark room
sun, moon and stars in the sky.
Chiaroscuro
You strike the balance
pulling me away from
my loneliness--
the cold, dark future
I envision for myself
toward a light that
kisses cheeks
dances across eyelids
moves from petal to petal
across fields and countries
shattering itself in a profusion of
gold garment
that wraps me
for an instant
like a flame.
So rich is life
that the shadows are
chasing this.

Transformation *by Margaret A. Dukes*

Bedrock along the highway

changed so much

in all my commutes.

Cut through to create an interstate

over 20 years ago

this once baldfaced hillside

today sprouts

trees, plants, shrubs

anchored in the sun.

Kiss of the Flower *by Frank Dworak*

Today I watched a flower grow
Shrinking time
In time lapsed photos
A pregnant bud with puckered lips
Peeled back its green and slowly
Spread petals of pink and red
Opening wide its mouth to reveal
Interior life and rows of anthers white.
Later, in the fading light
Tenderly it closed to say "Good Night."

Like the flower, I pursed my lips,
Imitating the flower's start,
Kissed the sky and slowly
Let lips spread until
My mouth was joy-fully open,
Revealing rows of pearly white,
Then gradually let lips seal it
To discovered what the flower spoke:
A slow-motion silent "WOW."

Beauty and the Beach *by Maryann Pennella*

It's coming. Can you hear it grumbling in the distance?

Today it's not the majestic beauty of a quiet orange sunset slipping into the water that brings applause from those on the shore.

An approaching storm is laying claim to its own performance commanding you to see its beauty as well. A light and sound symphony is in store.

The sky yields its pastural blue to a menacing shade of grey as the sun has taken shelter behind the pregnant clouds. The earth, water, wind and sky chat with each other as the palm trees begin their dance. The wind is their conductor as they twist and bend at the waist like an exercise routine.

The sky offers an explosion of energy as thunder pounds like a kettle drum Lightning flies across the sky resembling children fighting with glow sticks.

The once blue green water turns brown as sand coughs up from the bottom. The darkness of this huge body of water stretches to the horizon that accepts the setting sun most days. Waves move from gentle ripples to white foam anxious to crash on the shore.

Life teams below the water's surface. How does it stay anchored in the midst of so much turmoil? At times the wind doesn't seem to know when to stop roaring.

And then it happens. For a few riveting moments the skies explode and the rain slaps the water and the shore. Then the wind takes a breath, becomes a whisper and the sun comes out again.

The tension is over. It was a beautiful concert.

Time *by Joan Gunning*

The awaited birth was finally here
And we rejoiced
Time and patience delivered more
More than what could be imagined.

God created a beautiful little boy
Large blue eyes and golden hair.
We saw ourselves in him and smiled
Thanking God for this gift of love.
"Owen will be a fine Irishman full of stories to tell quick to smile and bring laughter and joy for all he meets."

Owen's Mission was filled with love
to help us understand that
Time was a fleeting experience

But love is Eternal.
It's not how long you stay but what is accomplished while here.
Owen needed but a short time
to complete his Mission of Everlasting: Love
Our smiling Irish boy is Home

Well of love *by Louise Easton*

An infinite well of love lies deep
in the center of my being

Resting bottomless within nature's womb

From where it was birthed in cadence with
universal life.

A dwelling place, a seedbed of individual
presence.

Hope stained walls carried by tides
of time record the endless flow of love that
nourishes my body, regularly refreshing
its parched kindness.

Rippling pearls often break a voyage silence.

Dancing in uneasiness as it seeks the softness
of this loving flow

That thwarts anger, releases resentment,
isolates fear.

While it fashions a new level for the journey to
begin again.

Faith and Grace at EAME *by Linda Stamato*

Virtuous people have wept openly
Have gathered in prayer and in protest
Have examined their consciences
Searched their souls
Have praised the forgiving.

Good people expressed
Awe at the faith, the fortitude.
Nine, their job on earth, buried,
Shot In a sanctified space where
Generosity and grace persist.

Searching people listen, heed words of
those close to the cherished nine.

Resolute people reject paralysis
when evil is persevered.

Peaceful people witness
The virtuous, the good, the searchers.

All are called to recall
To abolish ways and means
that incite violence.

Mother's Day Poem to the World *by Margaret Dukes*

    The wind swipes
    the sun hat
    off my head
    three times.
    I chase after it
    in the grass,
    wipe off
    accumulated
    specs of mulch.
    continue onward
    through the veterans
    housing complex
    for the no-longer
    homeless
    Crowns of white clouds
    remind me
    of the regal privilege
    we all share:
    each day to take
    delight in
    each other,
    in our shared
    or divergent paths
    here on
    Mother Earth

Cuckoo-bum-castle *by Fran Dworak*
Name-calling is hurtful to all.

She was trembling with anguish
This beautiful spirited sprite sobbed
"The boys called me a *cuckoo-bum-castle*
They are sooooo mean!"

A burst of bliss
A strong urge to giggle
Holding the laugher inside I found...
Her hurt touched, connected, fixed
Tears liberally fell from my eyes

My arms widened to invite an embrace
With a concerned smile, I held her,
hugged her, comforted her
till sleep overcame.

Poem of the Morning *by Margaret A. Dukes*

I want to fly
like the Blue Heron
with my fear flayed out
behind me
heading toward
the pond of plenty
where kindness swims
and I can see it
- catch it
- release it
at will.

Minds-Eye Wings *by Fran Dworak*

When I was six
I pirouetted in a tutu
Before Grandma and the rest
With the sugar plum fairy, I leapt high
With wings I flew

When I was twelve
At the recital before all the Grandmas
Gliding across the lit stage
Performing Peter Pan
I waved my lighted wand
Up high and away

Now I am a Grandma
Leotard warming my legs
On my mind's stage
I can hear, I can feel, I can see

I fly with the pathos of Tchaikovsky
My Odette arabesques reaching a
heavenly high as I glissade smoothly
across the wide lake, I am the swan
soaring on minds-eye wings

The Painter *by Pat Koman*

As I walked into the room of the cottage, I saw the painting hanging on the wall. What a magnificent piece of art – the vibrant colors, the sunlight and the shadows, and then I looked out the window in front of me and realized it was the before of the painting on the wall.
Beyond the lake the trees were bare and the ground was covered with dried leaves and small and large rock outcroppings. I was drawn to the window. What I saw was so dreary and yet the painting showed what might be.

Each morning I looked out the window with anticipation. Nothing seemed to be happening and then the light hues of pink and green appeared against the blue sky and bits of green came up through the leaves. I ventured out. Slowly the buds on the trees turned into flowers and leaves. Vines began to spread and the flowers appeared amongst the rocks. I could feel the warm breezes and smell the beautiful fragrances of the trees and flowers. The birds came and the sound was music. As I sat on the deck, I realized that I am a part of the living painting, and I know who the painter is.

On Seeing Warhol at the Whitney
by Julie O'Connell

Immediate Czech ghetto lightening
polished Pittsburgh brilliance
Illustrious
but shy
like my own sweet love.
He'd be the same age as my dad
(if he hadn't been shot,
that is), this
wigged artist
with the alabaster skin,
this fan magazine consumer
with the rheumatic fever brain
this mirror duplicator
making permutations
within the same.
It feels like print
this pop art, with its
blotted lines and thick colors
It feels stolen, this
art that is commerce that is art that is

commerce

framed with celebrity and glasses

thick and round as the bottoms of Coke bottles

"Everything is just how you decide

to think about it"

or speak about it

or see it in his

vernacular receptive reinventing mirror

reflecting us

prophesizing the Selfie revolution

projecting

tracing

seducing us with 32 types of soup

and the Velvet Underground

All of it passing through us like

paint on a silk screen.

Oregon Spring *by Don Kuhn*

Oregon rain

Ground soggy

Mists secreting mountain tops

Water standing in fields,

Rushing in roadside ditches.

A blue patch opens.

Rays appear

Like stage lights.

Still, rain splashes down.

Clouds move off

Wet leaves flash

Color intensifies:

Sage lichen

Olive cedars

Red, red madrone

Green, green grasses.

A pregnant world,

Absorbing, swelling,

About to burst,

Creates, renews, transforms

All life under this

Sheltering dome.

The Robins of Spring *by Frank Dworak*

Four robins squatted on my lawn
At corners of a fancied square
Watching me as I watched them
Competing in a game of "Stare."

I did not blink, I doubt they could,
Lacking lids to hide their eyes,
Long we stayed in frozen time,
Possum trances our disguise.

Had they hatched a secret plan
To build a nest atop my lamp
Where last year they left me straw
Woven tight, gone musty damp?

They broke the spell and broke the square
Hopped and stopped to hear the worms.
Ignoring their diversion tactics,
I kept guard, stood my ground firm.

How haughtily did these fragile birds
Proudly puffing their orange breasts
'Neath caps of black o'er beaks of gold
Regard this scarecrow a harmless pest.

She Walks with Grace *by Maureen Grant*

Like the arrival of spring,
She warms the earth with her love,
Awakens it with her spirit,
Cultivates it with her caring,
Moistens it with her tears,
Lightens it with her laughter and
Lifts it with her hope.

In the orbit of her love
We too reflect her radiance,
Celebrate life,
Embrace joy,
Dance and sing,
Snuggle and hug,
In one gracefilled circle of love.

The Flower of Spring *offered by Norman Lubeck*

Worthy words in today's news
Remind me of your sunlit face
A well-known poem about daffodils
Reports of seeing yellow crowds
High on hill and vale
Like you, dancing and glorifying
this cheerful spring day

Early Summer Day *by Don Kuhn*

The lake is mercurial:
Now, polished granite
As mists curl up,
Scrim to the surrounding trees.
Then, a breeze weaves herringbone v's
Like suiting unrolled by a tailor –
Greens, grays, and blues.
First rays touch down
Adding sequined ripples.
The day warms;
Mothers arrive with children
Whose squealing,
Splashing, tumbling
Delights.
Can they catch some minnows?
Will the fish nibble their toes?
Kayaks – blue, red, yellow –
Scrawl more complex lines
Moving up and down the surface.
On the beach, bodies stretch out.
Books, lotions, sunglasses
Spill from satchels.
The children's screams become white noise
To neighborhood gossip.

A veteran swimmer plunges in,
Churns across the lake
To a waiting dock.
Shadows inch toward the water,
Numbers thin until just two children
Persist in the fish chase.
Parents call them in.
The water levels,
Darkens, opaque,
Mysterious.

Meditation by the Pool *by Camille Yates*

The power of light from the Arizona sun
encompasses my body as heat radiates off
the webbing massaging my spine.
Poolside, I'm hearing sounds of splashing.
Children, parents chanting to their toddlers:
"Jump, you can do it."
I force myself to isolate, to ignore the frenzy.
After all, I am trying to meditate.

Focusing on my breath, I squeeze my eyes shut,
tight, but the noise distracts, it creeps back.
I tell myself: breathe in, breathe out.
Oh, oh, water droplets splashing upward,
shocking my arms, legs and face with sensations:
a hundred steel blades pierce the serene reverie.

Leaping upright, stiffened, my eyes pop open,
breath has quickened to an alarming pace, but then,
although startled, I grasp the delightful, the
life around me and surrender to observe the joy.
I realize mediation cannot bring this kind of bliss.
When thoughts are interrupted, I hear:
"Grandma, jump, you too can do it."
So I do!

Monsoon Listening by Susan Kraus

Two mockingbirds wait patiently
    On the fernlike Mesquite bough.
A throaty "check-check" to each other
    Akin to a tree frogs call.
    It breaks the silence all around
The peace that drizzling rain bestows
    on desert landscape.
    Heavy white shawls
    over mountain canyons
    Do not complain.

The sun did not wake me at six today
    Through my windows, it is gray.
    Only one mourning dove rests
    on top of the dead Acacia tree,
    Alone today on her favorite branch
    Just like me, her mate is
    sleeping in today.

No Thrasher's sharp "whit-wheet" call,
No Cactus Wren's harsh "cha cha cha"
No "Ho...Ho-Ho" of Gambel's Quail,
    To cue her that it's daybreak.
She need not share her cool rain bath
    And stretchy morning Yoga.

Digging Dahlias *by Don Kuhn*

After a final burst of energy and bloom
The dahlias hang limp, hit by the first frost.
Leaves, once shining and erect,
Hang like cooked spinach.
Yesterday, I cut the plants down,
Dug circles around them with my spade,
Lifted the tubers and set them out to dry
And then to store for the winter.
Today, my right hip reminds me
Of that digging, a twinge as I move about –
But a meager payment
For the glory those dahlias gave all summer.

Tucson Poem *by Susan Kraus*

Mountains shrouded in clouds
Do not complain.
Looking over the garden gate
South and West at the horizon
Four rocky mountain ranges
Are shielded from my view.
I squint: Do they exist?
This might be flat New Jersey,
Texas or New Hampshire.
Turning Northward, I greet with joy
My Tucson desert home.
Saguaro cactus standing tall
Mesquite and Palo Verde trees,
Growing rapidly in the mist.
Fuzzy black tarantula
Resting unbothered in the driveway.
Why worry....They're very shy.

Autumn Prayer *by Don Kuhn*

Dear Lord, you're the greatest! When efficiency and productivity call for standardization You decide to make everything a little -- or a lot different.

Sometimes, it's hard for us to see that. We know that we look different, but of course we assume that everybody else should think and feel just like we do. A walk in the woods at a time like this probably brings the point home better.

That magnificent maple at the edge of the field is pure butter yellow, all the leaves just the same hue. ---Or are they? Isn't there a tinge of rose on that lower branch? What about those tawny tans brushing against the dark greens of that chestnut oak that hasn't even thought of changing to its autumn brown?

The locusts all seem to act in a pack. They celebrate together and then on cue, take a bow, showering the earth with pennies, leaving their naked arms reaching for the sky. -- So different from their pin oak friends who hang on, hang on, hang on right through the blasts of winter.

Dogwoods, on the other hand, shake loose their russet mantle and, while the earliest to let go, leave bright red berries to say they were there.

The tulips are amazing, their huge leaves, like golden footprints walk across the forest floor as if daring anyone else to make a point. While the swamp maple has dropped a shaggy carpet of magenta and tan, ready to support anything than comes along.

The oaks, taking their time to turn mahogany, go one by one, the great individualists, ruggedly holding to one path, but maybe ending up on another.

Lord, we are those maples, locusts, dogwoods. We can dazzle, we can turn brown. We can hang on or let go, bend and dip, fly heavenward or straight to earth. We can be a symphony of color, a kaleidoscope chasing a dream. We can get sodden with a sudden shower, or turn moldy, settled into time-worn ruts.

All we ask is that you accept us as we are.
A patchwork quilt, blanketing the cooling earth, protecting the sleeping roots, we hope will welcome a new spring.

Winter Wonder *by Frank Dworak*

Bedded down beneath the down,
Awakened early by a sneeze,
I slip from bed, don slippers on
And stiffly straighten balky knees.

As I strain, to clear my brain
From mist that stole in through the night,
I peer through slats, Venetian blinds,
Finding only blinding white.

When blinking frees my eyes from haze
I find what freezing Winter weaves:
Coats of snow for fields below and
Wraps for woods with jeweled sleeves.

Everywhere, where'er I stare,
I see icy trees.

Late Autumn *by Margaret McCaffrey*

Gliding through late autumn days,
Surrounded by browns and grays of winter
I encounter the oaks,
Newly bared, insides showing, naked,
uncloaked. And the tree in me cries out,
Recognizing fragile sameness of our veins,
Sensing our like rootedness,
Souls planted in a fate
Determined by seeds scattered,
Sun. Rain.
Alone in lonely places called me,
Not free to leaves ourselves
We're bound to the land of pulsing patterns,
Cycled syndromes,
Defined, planned.
So we surrender to love's blazing smiles with
outward blindness,
Storing kindness on the sly,
All the while knowing that when cold times enter
We must stay,
Hang on to our centers,
Thankful that our roots go deep.
Sleep. Dream of warmth,
Beguiling scheme. Endless theme
Brighten your day.

Grand Old Oak Tree *by Fran Dworak*

Though old and gnarled - beautiful
the shadow of bare outstretched arms
falls on the flowers - on the stones
on the flags - sentinels standing in salute.
Sheltering revered loved ones, she reached out
a span wide and deep to her curious root tips.

As a youth her elbows coddled singing robins,
nesting noisy squirrels and little girls and boys
climbing vying for position there on her large
weathered bosom. She was the most pictorial
grand-mama of all, donning her winter coat,
spring white pearls, summer green hats and
bright orange autumn shoes.

Now It is time for poets for photographers,
time for a *last* photo to be clicked and added
to her grand album, time for the promise of an
acorn sprout planted tearfully, budding fresh
leaves in *her* enduring life's story.

I Wonder as I Wander *by Margaret McCaffrey*

On our march to the sun,
To the One?
At the logic behind Who lands where?
In what body? In which time?

Amazed. Dazed. Half crazed.
At what children we remain
As gypsy wanderings lead me through the miracle'd
maze.

Lost. Confused. Sadly unamused
By the nature of the game through which we dance.

Boys and girls growing older.
Playing parts chosen by chance.
Plot of the mysteried drama
never fully unfolded
to those who must keep wandering,
on their march to the sun.
To the One.

Endless scheme.
Beguiling dream.

One Lifetime *by Fran Dworak*

When at first light Eos wakes the horizon
Gracefully welcoming the unfolding
Revealing a claret heart drawing energy
Promised by heaven's radiating sphere
The fixed bond flows unseen
Calling forth a delicate fragrance

Now a stunningly illuminating beauty
Affirmed by a kaleidoscope of witnesses
Promoted by lush choruses
In a display of holy pageantry
The attentive bonded bouquet
Lives magically in the enriched sharing

Ah, the world turns on the day
The sky dyes to an enraptured red
Bonds held in agreement
Now break

The consummated hibiscus
Folds its filigreed petals
Accepting fate's transfer to Nyx
One earthly spin in time's measure

Made in the USA
Middletown, DE
14 May 2019